GW00670514

a year in the life of padstow, polzeath and rock

a year in the life of padstow, polzeath and rock

joanna jackson

To Ellen, Liz, Rosemary, Paula, Sharon, Jackie, Adele, Keh and Anna.
Thank you all for being such good friends.

Thanks to
Dom Boothroyd and staff at the Lobster Hatchery
Jane Myles
Ollie Myles and the lifeguards
Everyone at Prideaux Place especially Jean Hague who was so entertaining
Alan Tarby and Mike England at the Padstow Lifeboat station
Fenella and Martin at the Harlyn Inn
Liz and Rob Read
Mel and her family

TITLE PAGE Looking towards Padstow and Rock down the Camel Estuary at sunrise
HALF-TITLE PAGE Yachts anchored at Rock
BELOW Mediterranean coloured sea, looking towards Polzeath

Frances Lincoln Limited
4 Torriano Mews
Torriano Avenue
London NW5 2RZ
www.franceslincoln.com

A Year in the Life of Padstow, Polzeath and Rock

First Frances Lincoln edition 2010

[illegible] publication data
[illegible] this book is available from the British Library

[illegible] 112-2922-8

[illegible] in China

contents

introduction

The vast tracts of sand of the Doom Bar exposed at low tide, looking towards Daymer Bay

The town of Padstow nestles in a valley on the west side of the Camel Estuary. For 4000 years the area has been a trading port. From the Bronze Age onwards traders from Ireland travelled east and traders from the eastern Mediterranean travelled west. There are even some people who believe that Jesus spent some of his teenage years travelling in Cornwall possibly visiting Padstow! Later the already well trodden route between Padstow and Fowey linking Ireland with Brittany became known as the Saint's Way. The significance of the area arises from the fact that it is the only sheltered estuary on the north coast of south west England from west Cornwall to Devon. Travellers preferred to sail down the estuary, disembark and walk across to the south coast rather than sail round the dangerous waters of Land's End.

The port of Padstow thrived in Tudor times when Sir Walter Raleigh worked for Queen Elizabeth in the Old Custom House. The first stone pier was built in the sixteenth century. The importance of mining and quarrying in the area saw the port grow and fishing has always played a large part in the life of the town especially in the mid nineteenth century during the pilchard boom years. At that time there were six shipyards all busy building new vessels. As the mining industry declined many Cornishmen, women and children emigrated to Canada, leaving for their new life on ships departing from Padstow. The ships would return carrying timber for the ship building industry.

Last century tourism started to become important and visitor numbers have continued to grow ever since.

It is easy to see why the area is so popular. Polzeath on the east side of the estuary is perfectly placed to take advantage of the Atlantic waves and is a haven for surfers. Further down the east side of the estuary, Rock is loved by sailors and water skiers. Across from Rock, Padstow is still an active fishing port but it has retained its medieval and Elizabethan character, making it a charming place to visit. Rick Stein has put the town on the map as a place where it is possible to eat the very best seafood in the country and 'foodies' visit for long weekends all year round. The summer is the height of the tourist season however, with thousands flocking to enjoy the area. Whether you choose to walk the coast path, cycle the Camel Trail, surf, sail, eat or just relax it is the most wonderful place to be.

winter

Light on the sea

pre-history

In the 1980s strange marks appeared in the fields of the farm at Lellizzick, near Stepper Point. Aerial photos of the area taken by archaeologists revealed dozens of circular, semicircular shapes and lines running across the cliff top fields. Further excavation and investigation unearthed evidence of a major site occupied from the Bronze Age through the Iron Age.

Burial sites for the Beaker People, so called because when they were buried a beaker of water was placed at the head of the corpse, had already been found at Harlyn Bay. These people came from the Mediterranean area and knew how to make bronze. They brought this technique to the south west of England and found a plentiful supply of raw materials in the area with which to work. Tin was found lying as gravel in many streams and copper was visible as a green streak in rocky outcrops and cliffs. Bronze is made by combining the two metals. The Bronze Age began around 2000BC and it was a crucial period of pre-history linking the Stone Age to the Iron Age.

The Beaker People mixed freely with the Neolithic Stone Age farmers who already inhabited the area and had been responsible for planting the first Cornish hedges that are now such an integral part of the county's scenery.

The Bronze Age settlement at Crugmeer is considered to be an ancient trading centre. Originally gold from Ireland and later the bronze from Cornwall were taken along a packhorse trail from Padstow to Fowey on the south coast and onward to northern France and the Mediterranean. In the opposite direction Phoenicians, Egyptians and Greeks brought oil, wine and pottery to Cornwall. This route later became known as the Saint's Way.

The Bronze Age gave way to the Iron Age which in Britain was considered to be from 700BC to 43AD. Iron was introduced to Britain by the Celts. In the 1970s an Iron Age fort was excavated at The Rumps. From the air, ramparts can be clearly seen stretching across the narrow isthmus which links the twin headlands to the mainland. It is possible that this was a summer fort because in the winter it would have been an incredibly exposed site with fierce gales battering the area. The Veneti tribe that lived there had an extensive fleet of trading vessels.

These two habitations have straddled the Camel Estuary for 4000 years trading with Ireland and France and Wales. The Celtic culture of Cornwall and its language have their origins in this era.

LEFT Winter surfer
RIGHT Homeward bound, Constantine Bay

OPPOSITE
TOP Harlyn Bay at dusk
BOTTOM Mist over the rocks

BELOW Tide out at Daymer Bay

the dark ages (the age of the saints)

Sign posts for the Saint's Way. A walk from Padstow to Fowey retracing the steps of the medieval saints

The Romans lived in Britain for roughly 400 years from about 43AD to 409AD. They didn't set up permanent settlements of any importance in Cornwall but there is plenty of evidence of mutual trading. Two hill forts have been found, one at Nastallon, in the middle of Cornwall near Bodmin, the other near Restormel Castle. These are both on the Fowey/Camel River trade and communication route now known as the Saint's Way and show that this route was of significant enough importance to warrant defending. Roman jewellery has been found at Rock, items which were likely to have been acquired through trade.

Around 409AD, the Romans began to have trouble with other parts of their Empire and withdrew their troops from England to deal with the uprisings in mainland Europe. This enabled tribes of Jutes, Saxons, Franks and Angles to invade England. These were heathen tribes who paid scant regard to the niceties of the Roman civilisation left behind as a legacy of occupation. The British appealed for help from their old invaders. Their appeal fell on deaf ears as the Romans were engaged in desperately fighting to cling onto the last vestiges of their once glorious empire.

So began the Dark Ages.

When the heathen hoards invaded southern England the Romano-Britains fled west from Angle Land (England) to Wales and Cornwall. The Saxons then dominated southern England for the next 600 years until the arrival of the Normans. However they struggled to completely control Western Dumnonia, the area west of Dartmoor, now west Devon and Cornwall. This was the era of the Saints and the Western Kings. The Celtic tribes united to halt the western expansion of the Angles and Saxons with the British (Brythonic Celts) fighting off the English (Angles)! The legendary King Arthur was supposedly a warrior defending the west of England. There may be some small amount of truth in the stories but most of it is myth and fantasy.

At about this time monks from Ireland and Wales began entering Cornwall spreading their Celtic Christianity through the land in a period known as 'The Age of the Saints'. The saints exercised a religious and political influence being closely connected to the civil rulers. One such saint was Petroc who had enormous influence over the shaping of Padstow.

St. Petroc was the son of a Welsh prince. He was educated in Ireland which in the sixth century was important for its great religious centres. He set sail from Ireland accompanied by monks to spread the Christian faith. They let the wind take their boat where it wanted believing that it was God's will where they landed. That wind happened to take them down the Camel Estuary and they landed in Trebetherick. The group then crossed the Camel and built Padstow's first church and an accompanying monastery.

St. Petroc travelled widely, spending time in Brittany, Rome and possibly Jerusalem. As a sick old man he travelled back to his monastery in Padstow but never quite made it, dying at Treravel farm on the outskirts of the town. He was buried in Padstow which became a place of pilgrimage and the ecclesiastical capital of Cornwall. The monastery remained important until it was ransacked by the Vikings in 981AD.

There is a lasting legacy from this time when St. Petroc and his fellow saints were so influential. The church in Padstow is called St. Petroc's and it stands in more or less the same place as when it was first built. Two Celtic crosses from that time remain in the churchyard. The name Padstow is a derivation of one of its former names 'St. Petrocstowe' and similarly Little Petherick means St. Petroc minor. St. Petroc put Padstow on the map in the sixth century and it has been there ever since.

BELOW Watergate bay

OVERLEAF Waves batter the coast at Treyarnon

Wind and waves at Harlyn Bay

Late light at Trevose Head

Stormy Treyarnon

Polzeath Beach at dusk

LEFT Lobster pots on the quayside at Padstow, looking across the estuary to Rock
BELOW Padstow harbour

RIGHT Lobster pots collected on the quayside awaiting repair over the winter months
BELOW Fishing boats, Padstow harbour

Swans glide silently on the calm waters of the Camel Estuary

The view towards the obelisk over the fields from the top of the hill near Tesco in Padstow

Sunrise over the Camel Estuary

Sunset looking from Portilly
towards the obelisk

Tide in at sunset,
Daymer Bay

foodie padstow

Rick Stein signs books for adoring fans at his Deli in Padstow

Annually, at the beginning of December, Padstow holds a Christmas festival. It lasts for four days and culminates in a firework display, exploding rockets reflected dramatically in the calm water of the inner harbour. During the festival the town celebrates its reputation as a 'foodie' destination. Every afternoon in the memorial hall the talented chefs of the local restaurants put on cookery demonstrations where eager would-be chefs watch in awe as maestros cook delicious offererings. Tasting after the demonstrations is obligatory. There are also local beers, wines and cheeses on offer to try. Many of the local restaurants offer themed meals and aromas of hog roasts fill the evening air, as shoppers meander around the narrow streets taking advantage of the late night shopping opportunities whilst sipping hot mulled wine.

Padstow was put on the 'foodie' map by the fame and success of local restauranteur and celebrity chef Rick Stein. Having always holidayed in the area as a child he moved to Padstow in the early 1970s and set up a nightclub with his future wife. It was a rowdy place on a Saturday night. Fights at the end of the evening were the norm rather than the exception and as a result the police shut the place down. Due to an oversight though, only the entertainment licence was revoked while the restaurant licence remained, so the enterprising couple opened a restaurant instead. This became *The Seafood Restaurant* and it opened in 1977. In 1984 it was voted Egon Ronay's restaurant of the year. It was doing reasonably well even then but when Rick got his own TV cookery series "A Taste of the Sea" in 1993 it really took off as the place to eat and has been packed ever since.

As Rick's TV career grew so did his Padstow empire. He and his now ex-wife currently own four more restaurants, *Stein's Fish & Chips*, *Rick Stein's Café*, *St. Petroc's Bistro* and a pub in nearby St. Merryn called *The Cornish Arms*. Add to those the deli, the patisserie, the gift shop, *Padstow Seafood School* and the factory on a local trading estate making bespoke chutneys etc. and you can begin to see how the name 'Padstein' came about. His success has led to the improved standard of all the restaurants in the town. Many of his ex-chefs have opened up rival establishments and anyone who likes a fine dining experience is spoilt for choice when visiting. Padstow's proximity to the sea lends itself to good quality fresh fish cooking but it is also surrounded by farms producing high quality meat and vegetables so all ingredients can be locally sourced. Padstow truly is a fabulous destination for a dedicated 'foodie'.

Fishing boats in the harbour at night

Fireworks celebrate the Christmas festival, held in Padstow in December

Ready for the pot – brown crab and
wonderful mackeral, fresh from the sea

On a frosty morning the inner harbour was covered in ice and weird ice formations on the wire struts of the harbour gates were beginning to melt as the sun rose

Ice on the calm waters of Padstow harbour is a rare event

Come rain or shine there is always time to practice gig racing

An unusual sight — frost on the beach

Incredibly calm water. Looking towards
Padstow from the low water ferry slipway

Flying popcorn or seafoam?
Treyarnon after a stormy night

spring

Sea and sky

'obby 'oss day

To the people of Padstow 'Obby 'oss day is hugely important. They return to their home town from all over the world to celebrate. Over the years there have been attempts to stop the event due to rowdiness but these have always failed and it remains one of the oldest traditions still celebrated in the UK.

The celebrations kick off at midnight on the 30th April with the assembled crowd outside the Golden Lion public house, stable to the 'old 'oss'. They start to sing:

'Unite and unite, and let us all unite
For summer is a-come unto day and whither we are
Going we all will unite in the merry morning of May'

The singers wander around the town singing for the next few hours. In the morning the locals don their white trousers and shirts and adorn themselves with either the blue ribbons of the blue ribbon 'oss or the red of the old 'oss. Cowslips and bluebells are added for effect into button holes, belts and hats. The blue ribbon 'oss emerges at ten in the morning from the town institute and an hour later, the old 'oss emerges from the Golden Lion. They both make their way around town, following different routes, accompanied by bands of accordionists and drummers, singing traditional songs. The 'oss swirls around being led by the prancing teaser. They meet at the end of the day by the Maypole for more communal dancing and singing before being put back in their stables for another year.

The day's origins are interesting, but over time have become muddled. What is known is that May Day has been celebrated across Europe for time immemorial. The ancient pagan Celts celebrated 1st May with the festival of Beltane. Bel was the Celtic god of the sun and Beltane meant 'fires of god'. The festival celebrated the coming of the summer and fertility of the coming year. Rituals included young men and women collecting blossoms and lighting fires in the evening. These rituals would often lead to marriage. The celebrations became entwined with the May Queen and The Greenman, ancient god and goddess figures representing fertility and growth, the latter evolving into the legendary figure Robin Hood. The Maypole was a phallic symbol around which the young single men and women of the village would dance holding onto ribbons until they became entwined with hopefully a new love.

The Morris Men are also an integral part of the story. Morris dances are thought to be of Indo-European origins because of the wide distribution of such similar dances. There are examples of dancers wearing white clothes and with bells attached all over Europe, the Middle East, India and even parts of Central and South America. It is believed that the Morris dancing traditions were introduced to England by John of Gaunt in the fourteenth century when he returned from Spain, having fought for the Christians against the Muslim Moors. Morris is considered to be a derivation of the word Moorish. The dances often had a central figure, usually an animal man, in some cases he dominated the dance. Such is the case in Padstow. The 'oss is always black, a colour associated with fertility, and it used to be considered that if the 'oss caught a female she would become pregnant. Thus the single young maidens would run from the rampant 'oss.

As with many Pagan traditions, aspects of the rituals were incorporated in later Christian festivities. The Celtic Mayday festival morphed into the Christian Mayday festival. In Europe the Catholic Church outlawed Mayday celebrations but many ignored the papal declarations and continued to celebrate. In England the Puritan government of Oliver Cromwell also tried to put a stop to the revelleries and banned the use of Maypoles, all to no avail.

In Padstow in the early 1900s the Mayday antics were certainly seen by some as unacceptable. Thomas Tregaskis, a local merchant, farmer and preacher attempted to divert the revellers from following the 'oss by offering to roast a bullock for their consumption. The Mayers declined his offer. 50 years later at the turn of the nineteenth century the event was being described as 'a very rough and coarse pastime' and 'a relic of barbarism'.

The whole event has survived setbacks and changes and continues to evolve occurring annually, unabated, and ever more popular. Long may it continue as part of our fascinating national heritage and Padstow's special day.

OPPOSITE Young and old all celebrate 'obby 'oss day in Padstow, with two bands marching around the town led by their teaser and 'oss

BELOW The decorated Maypole

Early morning ferry to Rock. The ferry between Rock and Padstow sails all year round

Padstow at dawn

The town at dusk from the iron bridge

egg rolling

Every Easter sees the children of Padstow congregate at the top of the hill on Duke Street, decorated hardboiled eggs in hand, ready to roll their eggs down the slope as fast as they can. This is the annual egg rolling competition. When they eventually reach the bottom, the eggs, if they have made it at all, are usually in a pretty sorry state. Bits of hardboiled egg litter the road and the air is full of the smell of eggs! The children however are happy because they collect a chocolate egg at the finish.

Easter was originally a pagan festival celebrating the spring equinox on March 21st and named after the goddess of spring Eostre. Her animal was the hare and the rebirth of the land in spring was symbolised by the egg. After the coming of Christianity Pope Gregory the Great ordered his missionaries to absorb old religious festivals into Christian rituals wherever possible. It is believed that the egg rolling tradition at Easter is symbolic of the rolling away of the rock from Jesus' tomb before his resurrection.

This tradition was taken to the United States with the early European settlers and every year there is an egg rolling event on the lawn of The White House. In the UK egg rolling events take place all over the country. Traditionally the egg rolling was accompanied by mumming plays, the singing of songs and the collecting of money. In Padstow the collecting of money is the only tradition that survives and all collections are donated to the worthy RNLI.

LEFT The children roll decorated eggs down Duke Street, a charitable event in aid of the RNLI.
RIGHT Cleaning up all the hard boiled egg remains!

The view down Little Petherick Creek from the obelisk

Early morning ploughing

LEFT Cows and gorse on the Saint's way near the obelisk

OPPOSITE Walking the coast path with mum

surfing

LEFT Surfers in competition

OPPOSITE A keen junior surfer runs into the cold water

'Twenty or thirty of the natives, taking each a long, narrow board, rounded at the ends, set out together from the shore. I could not help concluding this man felt the most supreme pleasure while he was driven so fast and so smoothly by the sea' so wrote Captain James Cook in his ship's diary in 1778. He was in Hawaii and this was the first ever description of surfing. He and his crew were the first Westerners to view this activity which nearly 250 years later would be a worldwide sport enjoyed by an estimated twenty million people.

Surfing was the preserve of the Hawaiians until the beginning of the twentieth century. Then, with the advent of tourism, tales of this sport were taken back to California, and America started to catch the surfing bug. Its popularity grew slowly but steadily until in 1959 a Viennese émigré named Frederick Kohner wrote a best selling book called *Gidget* about his daughters' exploits surfing one summer in Malibu. This book was turned into an equally successful film. Coupled with the music of the Beach Boys, this transformed surfing from a sport for die-hards and life guards into a slightly anti-establishment movement. The image conscious young of the day began to buy into the whole lifestyle as much as the thrill of the surf. Participants grew from five thousand worldwide in 1959 to two million in 1963.

Back in the UK people had been riding the waves on converted coffin lids called belly boards since the early 1900s. Edward, the Prince of Wales, visited Hawaii in 1920. The Prince was given surfing lessons by 'The Duke'. Duke Kahanamoku was a Hawaiian Olympic gold medal swimmer. He was also a brilliant surfer and a glamorous figure who had been responsible for raising the profile of surfing in America. Back in 1960s Britain two sets of surfers had set up small communities in Newquay and St Quen, Jersey. They got together and started having competitions forming the British Surfing Association.

However, the trouble with surfing in Britain was the temperature. Only in the summer was it possible to surf for any amount of time as during the rest of the year the freezing conditions restricted activity. They tried wearing oiled woollen jumpers but these only delayed the inevitable numbness for a few minutes more – then came the neoprene revolution.

The 'father of the modern wetsuit' is commonly recognised as Hugh Bradner who realised that a thin layer of trapped water could act as an insulator. He wrote about this idea but never followed it up. It took the surfing O'Neil brothers Jack and Robert from California to design and make the first wetsuit in the 1950s with their catch phrase 'It's always summer on the inside'. Neoprene was a good insulator and buoyant but the early suits were stiff and uncomfortable and prone to tearing when taken on and off. In fact these tough surfers had to cover themselves in talcum powder to assist with getting into the wetsuit. Technology moved on though and with the development of nylon lining the suits became much more manageable. Today they have nylon on the inside and outside which enables the suits to be colourful and covered in logos and they are incredibly flexible compared to the original prototypes. Different thicknesses can be worn at different times of the year making year round surfing a possibility on our chilly coasts. The wetsuit has transformed surfing in the UK.

Polzeath is the big surf beach on the Camel Estuary. Its open west facing beach ensures big swells and good conditions when the wind is in the right direction. If the surf isn't so good in Polzeath, decent waves are usually to be found in the south west facing Harlyn Bay or further down the coast.

The link between surfing and the lifestyle it engenders continues today. Every few years a new film comes out that targets the next generation of surfers who are a marketing dream, spending a fortune getting 'the look'. In the meantime the beaches are getting more and more crowded and with no 'give way' rules on the waves tempers are rising. No doubt if the numbers surfing our beaches continues to rise rules will eventually have to be brought in as they have on the ski slopes. Surfing will have become a victim of its own success.

rip curl

Bluebells and wild garlic in Polbrook

the camel estuary

LEFT Puffin feeding on sand eels. They are fleeting visitors, staying only long enough to lay their eggs and bring up their young before returning to sea.

OPPOSITE
TOP A turnstone and a shag in the harbour, both becoming used to people being nearby
BOTTOM A little egret in Little Petherick Creek

Before the advent of engines in boats, sailors had to rely on the wind as their only means of propulsion. In stormy weather sailors on the north coast of Cornwall had few safe ports to hole up in and sit out bad weather. The Camel Estuary seemed such a safe haven. The Atlantic rollers and the fierce south westerlies would guide the ships down the estuary. Suddenly the wind would drop and without any other means of steering, the ships would be thrust onto the enormous sand bar that marks the entrance to the estuary. This stretch of sand, aptly named Doom Bar, has claimed over 300 ships in the last 150 years including three lifeboats. Legend has it that a beautiful mermaid was shot by a sailor and as she was dying she cursed the area so that the sand would continuously build up and provide a hazard to ships forever.

The estuary is five miles long and is tidal until it reaches Egloshayle just past Wadebridge. It is designated as one of only forty 'Areas of Outstanding Beauty' in the UK and it is truly magnificent. It is abundant with wildlife, the mud providing numerous different types of wading birds with a hearty meal. The haunting cry of the curlew can always be heard at dawn and dusk along with the calls of oyster catchers, redshanks and plovers. Flocks of dunlins visit in the winter and egrets, herons, cormorants, shags and turnstones are ever present. It is a birdwatcher's dream.

In the summer dolphins frolic in the waves, chasing motor boats and the lucky few might glimpse passing basking sharks. Grey seals come and go and a trip on *The Jubilee Queen* usually includes a sighting of some seals. Atlantic salmon and sea trout come up the estuary to get to their spawning grounds further up river and otters have been spotted as far down as the disused slate mines just outside Padstow. It is a significant breeding site for sea bass and as such is protected. Fishing for bass is only allowed at certain times of the year and they have to be a certain size or should be released back into the water. Oysters are harvested at an oyster farm at Portilly and millions of cockles can be seen glistening in the sun at low tide. People can often be spotted digging for lug worms (used as fishing bait).

The Camel River rises thirty miles away at Hendraburnick Down on Bodmin Moor. Along with its tributaries it drains a large part of north Cornwall. The water is clean and fresh and the river and estuary provide a fantastic environment for a diverse array of flora and fauna. Because of its value to the environment the area has many different government bodies protecting it. The river has along its course five 'Sites of Special Scientific Interest' and the whole area is considered worthy of the protection as a 'Special Area of Conservation'. This is an EU directive and as one of only seventy-eight similar sites in the UK, it gained this high level protection because of the presence of internationally important populations of Atlantic salmon, otters and bullheads (endangered fish).

The views of the estuary from Stepper Point and Pentire Point are spectacular and it is possible to walk the coast path from one point to the other crossing the water from Padstow to Rock on the Blackrock ferry which runs throughout the year. The Camel Trail follows the estuary from Padstow to Wadebridge and follows the river all the way to Bodmin so there is no excuse not to explore this amazing area.

A seaweed wall

Colourful purple and green rocks between Daymer Bay and Polzeath

Eerie windswept trees at Crugmeer

Trevose Head at sunset from Pentire Point

tourism, railways and the camel trail

Bathing in a sea mist

'A very commodious bathing machine is fitted for the accommodation of ladies and gents at the pleasant and healthy seaport town of Padstow'. So ran an advert in May 1792 encouraging the first tourists to visit Padstow. Up until that time Cornwall had been virtually cut off from the rest of England but with the advent of improved roads and better, more comfortable coaches people began to venture further west, first for business and later for pleasure.

However, tourists were relatively thin on the ground until the arrival of the railways at the end of the nineteenth century and when reading descriptions of the state of the town in the 1800s it is not surprising. A health inspector in 1850 gave the town a damning report. The town's sanitation was non-existent, many of the small back gardens housed pigs and swill and sewage ran freely down the narrow streets. It was little wonder that a cholera epidemic wiped out five percent of the population at that time. Sir Charles Prideaux-Brune was so disturbed by the deaths of so many people especially children that he installed main drains which greatly improved the conditions.

The first train arrived in March 1899. There had been a train from Wadebridge to Bodmin since 1834. This was predominantly built for the transportation of sand around the country. The sand extracted from the Camel Estuary was sold as agricultural fertiliser used for liming fields, providing good conditions for growing cabbages. The Camel Estuary sand is still sold for the same purpose today. There was talk of a line extension from Wadebidge to Padstow for many years but the route could not be decided on. Eventually it was decided that it would be best to follow the Camel River to the sea and so the most beautiful stretch of railway in the country was built. This route was known as the Atlantic Coast Express and Padstow station was the end of the line. At about the same time the South Western Hotel, now the Metropole, was built. This provided smart new accommodation for the rising numbers of summer visitors. Between the wars wealthy people from south west London were the most frequent holiday makers. After the Second World War the less wealthy arrived lured by the newly built caravan sites. The sixties saw the demise of the railways with Dr. Beeching's stringent cut backs. The Atlantic Coast Express was one such line. The last train chugged out of Padstow in January 1967.

Tourists with newly acquired cars still continued to visit the town but the railway line fell into disrepair. There were lots of ideas about what to do with it but nothing happened. The iron bridge across Little Petherick creek became dangerous. Eventually someone came up with the idea of a walking path which opened in 1980 and morphed into a cycling and walking path. This has now become a major attraction as tourists from all over Cornwall visit Padstow for the day to cycle the Camel Trail. It is possible to cycle the seventeen miles to Bodmin along the whole of the beautiful Camel River. There are plenty of places to stop and take on a variety of refreshments and a variety of wildlife to watch. Padstow and Wadebridge both have numerous cycle hire shops and both towns are awash with bikes on a hot summer's day. Although the loss of the railway dramatically affected Padstow, the Camel Trail now provides a source of enjoyment and income for many people.

In the 1851 edition of *Murray's Handbook of Devon and Cornwall* it describes Padstow as 'one of those antiquated, unsavoury fishing towns which are viewed most agreeably from a distance'. The author would be hard pushed to recognise the Padstow of today from that description.

Parked bikes ready to travel the camel trail

summer

farming and the royal cornwall show

Each year at the beginning of June over one hundred thousand people visit Wadebridge to enjoy the Royal Cornwall Show, a three day extravaganza of all things agricultural plus much more. It is the most important event in the year for many of Cornwall's residents as well as being a fun day out for many tourists. Cornwall is a very rural county with farming being one of the primary industries. This show is an opportunity for showing off your prize bull and to get together with fellow farmers for a jolly good gossip.

The first show was in 1793 organised by the Royal Cornwall Agricultural Association and consisted of a ploughing match between rival farmers. This was successful and the next year there were also prizes given for the fattest sheep (dead or alive) and other livestock awards. The show has been an annual event, apart from during the world wars, ever since. It used to be held in different locations, one year in the east and one in the west of the county but since 1960 its home has been at the Royal County showground in Wadebridge.

A farmer's lot is not an easy one. Over the last twenty years they have had to contend with foot and mouth, blue tongue, BSE and EU directives reducing the milk yields allowed. Because of the milk yields issue many dairy farms have struggled to make ends meet and have switched to beef cattle or have embraced tourism and turned farm cottages into holiday lets.

Carruan farm in Polzeath is an example of how the modern farm is changing. It is thriving since it decided to diversify. It is still a working farm but has a farm shop, holds daily events in the summer season such as sheep races and hog roasts and rents out fields for events such as Beach Breaks Live and touring theatre groups. Many of the farms on the coast work in conjunction with the National Trust, RSPB and other conservation bodies and are signed up to the Countryside Stewardship Scheme. This means they farm in an environmentally friendly way. Field margins are left uncultivated and no sprays or fertilizers are used. Hedgerows are maintained providing vital wildlife corridors, mixed farming is practiced and stubble is left in fields over winter. All these measures have been introduced to counteract the intensive farming practices of the 1980s and 1990s which saw more than a seventy percent decline in corn bunting and skylark populations and the decline of barn owls, grey partridge and hares. These are relatively new measures but research indicates that they are having a positive effect and figures are recovering slightly.

The whole of Cornwall sets a fine example to the rest of the country with its farming practices. Good quality locally grown seasonal produce with a low carbon footprint reared or grown in an environmentally friendly way is the way forward in these times of climate change. It might be a little more expensive but it's worth it in the long run.

The Royal Cornwall Show gives farmers the chance to show off their best livestock as well as having lots of other attractions for the general public to enjoy.

The cliff tops abundant with wildflowers such as thrift, sea campion and foxgloves

The classic view of the Camel Estuary towards Stepper and Pentire Points and the sea beyond

Towards Polzeath from Pentire Point

Mother Ivey's Bay

Towards Padstow from Pentire Point

The Rumps

Across the fields to Padstow

Bedruthan Steps

ABOVE Polzeath in the sunshine
LEFT Across the Camel Estuary to Rock

RNLI beach lifeguards

LEFT The common sight of windbreaks on the beach
RIGHT An RNLI lifeguard keeps his eye on the bathers

OPPOSITE Red and yellow flags mean it's safe to go in the water

All the main beaches around Padstow are manned by people dressed in distinctive red shorts and yellow shirts. Their trendy exterior should not distract from the fact that these are highly trained members of the rescue services and when they ask you not to swim outside the flags there is a very good reason for it and you ignore them at your peril!

Most lifeguards come from two distinct backgrounds, the surfers and the surf clubbers. The latter join surf clubs when young and compete against other clubs and in big competitions in various disciplines such as surf swimming or beach running, all based on the techniques learnt to help save lives. They are usually locals who know the beaches and sea in their area intimately. Like the surfers, they use the dangerous rip currents to their advantage to get them away from the beach to the big waves. They understand the sea and respect it.

All the beaches in the area are different. Harlyn and Polzeath are considered the safest, Constantine definitely the most dangerous. When the sea is really busy it is impossible to watch everyone. The lifeguards look for changes in the sea. They know the danger areas and signs and try to make sure the bathers don't go near them.

A rip current is caused when a section of soft soggy sand collapses leaving a channel of deeper water that funnels the water back out to sea. The water in that channel travels out to sea away from the beach faster than the surrounding water. The tell tale sign is an area of flat water. Just the sort of water you might think was the safest if you didn't understand the sea. Treyarnon and Trevone have distinctive rips that if you know what to look for are obvious; Harlyn has a constant rip to the right hand side of the beach well away from the flags; Polzeath has a big swell and waves but like Harlyn is relatively safe. It is Constantine's soft unstable sand that makes the beach so dangerous. Rips come and go in no particular pattern making conditions unpredictable.

The life guards go on duty at ten in the morning and their first task is to put the flags out. The state of the sea has to be assessed and the most appropriate flag chosen for the prevailing conditions. If the conditions are dangerous the red flags go out meaning no bathing, if it is safe to swim the red and yellow flags go out. They then have to keep the public in the safe areas – not always an easy task! It is the people who ignore their sensible advice that usually later have to be rescued. They stay on the beach until six in the evening. The season starts on 1st May and ends on most beaches on 30th September.

Surf lifesaving originated in Australia in the early 1900s. The growth of seaside towns and tourism led to several drownings. Local communities formed patrols alerting visitors to the dangers of the surf. In the UK the Surf Lifesaving Association was formed in 1955 when volunteer clubs first patrolled beaches in Bude and St Agnes. Over the years the number of beaches patrolled has steadily increased and over the last fifty years there have been over 20,000 rescues. The modern day training is rigorous and overseen by the RNLI who also maintain the huts and provide all the equipment. The local councils pay the wages. Come the winter many of the lifeguards travel south to Australia and New Zealand to take up lifeguarding jobs there.

Along with the coastguards and the lifeboatmen they make up the emergency services that patrol our cliffs, beaches and sea making them a safer place for us to enjoy.

Teeing off on the first at Trevose golf club

OPPOSITE Running and jumping on the sand dunes is all part of the fun of the beaches

Amazing sunset at Trevone

water sports

If you like messing about in the water there is no better place to go than the Camel Estuary. Every type of water sport that you can possibly imagine is catered for.

There are two sailing clubs on the estuary – a large one at Rock and a smaller one in Padstow. Both clubs are mainly for dingy sailors with the boats being 'laid up' or taken out of the water in October and popped back in around Easter time. Many people bring their boats with them on holiday so the number moored on the water in the summer can be enormous. The Rock club has many races and regattas throughout the season and it is fun to watch the boats tussling for position as they round the buoys trying to outwit each other, making the best use of the wind. The Padstow club is less competitive but very sociable. They have flotillas of boats at high tide which sail up to Wadebridge on a fish and chip run (sail to Wadebridge eat your fish and chips and sail back) and communal day sails often to Port Isaac (sail to Port Isaac have a pub lunch and sail back). These events are open to non members to get a taste of sailing and lessons are also available. So both recreational sailing and competitive sailing are on offer. In the summer the harbour also sees the arrival of lots of large, expensive ocean going touring yachts that moor in Padstow harbour for a couple of nights before setting off to their next port of call.

The Rock sailing club also has a water skiing club attached to it. There is a designated area in a sheltered part of the estuary for sole use of the wake boarders and water skiers. For safety reasons waterskiing is not allowed elsewhere. The club has its own boats and lessons can be booked. Many people have their own motor boats and in high season there is a constant stream of skiers and wake boarders whizzing up and down the estuary showing off their skills to the cyclists peddling along the nearby Camel Trail. A banana boat also frolics up and down and squawks of pleasure can be heard as the riders fall off.

If sailing or water skiing are not your idea of fun then move up the estuary to Daymer Bay. Here the windsurfers and kite surfers congregate. They career backwards and forwards between Tregirls Beach and Daymer Beach using the waves as a launch pad to take off and fly through the air. It is very dramatic to watch and looks exhausting.

Even further up the estuary is the surfing beach at Polzeath. The Atlantic rollers provide perfect conditions for surfers and body boarders alike to pursue their sport. In the summer the beach is packed with people enjoying the waves and then in the autumn when the bigger waves start appearing the serious year-round surfers really get going.

Sea kayaking is becoming increasingly popular and is a good alternative activity when the sea is flat and surfing is not possible. The kayaks can take you up river to view the wildlife and explore the creeks or further out to sea to explore the caves and coastline.

The latest extreme sport to hit the area is coasteering. This is the exploration of the coast doing a bit of climbing, a bit of swimming though white water, a bit of exploring caves and last but not least jumping into the sea from the cliffs.

All these activities are available in a very small area and are fun to do even if it is raining as you are going to get wet anyway! It is easy to see why the area is so popular.

Wake boarding, coasteering, kite surfing, windsurfing, body boarding and surfing – some of the many watersports on offer in the Camel Estuary

In the summer luxury yachts moor up in Padstow harbour

the padstow lifeboat

The annual RNLI day gives the opportunity for the combined rescue services to show off their skills

A mayday call goes out from a pleasure boat with 150 tourists on board that there has been an explosion in the engine room. There are many casualties and there is a danger that the boat might sink. The Falmouth coastguard picks up the signal, assesses the magnitude of the incident and sends out alerts to the emergency services. The Padstow lifeboat is the nearest to the disaster. Twenty five voluntary crew members and the local caravan sites are paged. Seven lifeboat men are needed to launch the boat. The caravan site employees act as road marshals clearing the road up to the lifeboat station so the crew members can get there as quickly as possible. The average time to launch from the time of the first page is an amazing ten minutes. The scenario described above was just one of the many regular training exercises that are carried out by the Padstow lifeboat and also involved the RAF helicopters and the local lifeguards. On average there are two emergencies a month that are real and that require the crew to be scrambled and sent out, often in appalling conditions to rescue seafarers in distress.

The RNLI is the charity that runs the lifeboat service using donations from the general public. The Padstow lifeboat station has two fulltime staff. The cox Alan Tarby who has been a lifeboat man for over thirty years, sixteen years part time and the last fifteen years as the full time cox and Mike England, the mechanic, whose father was the cox before Alan. Both were fishermen before becoming full time lifeboat men. Many of the other volunteer crew members are fishermen but there are also builders, publicans, students. What unites them is their love for and respect of the sea.

There has been a lifeboat at Padstow since 1827. Money was raised for the boat by a local man, Commander Williams, who was chief officer of the coastguard. 'The National Institute for the Preservation of Life from Shipwreck', the precursor of the RNLI, donated ten pounds which added to the thirty already collected. This was enough to build the first lifeboat *The Mariner's Friend* and a lifeboat station at Hawkers Cove. The original lifeboat men wore no lifejackets. It wasn't until 1854 that the crews were issued with cumbersome jackets made of corks.

For the first seventy years of its existence the men had to row out to any stricken vessels and sometimes it was too difficult to row past Stepper Point. On such occasions the overland route was used. This meant mobilising not only the crew but also the local farmers. A rocket would go up and the crew would run the one and a half miles to the lifeboat station. They would then row the boat to the town where they would meet the local farmers who had brought a carriage and eight horses to the harbour. The boat was loaded on the carriage and driven three miles to Harlyn Bay. They then launched the boat and rowed to the endangered craft. Such a rescue took place in 1872 in Trevone Bay when the lifeboat managed to save five crew members and the captain's wife and child from a ship that eventually broke up and sank.

In the 1960s the sand shifted from the Polzeath side to the Padstow side of the estuary. This left the channel to the harbour a long way away from the lifeboat station at low tide, making it difficult to launch the boat. It was decided to build a new station at Mother Ivey's Bay near Trevose Head. It is possible to launch the boat into all levels of the tide from this site. The new station was opened in 1968 and has recently been refurbished and is now a state of the art station and receives many visitors who drop in to read about the history of the Padstow lifeboat whilst walking the coast path. They always receive a warm welcome from crew on duty.

Over the years the boat has performed many rescues and saved many lives but two rescues stand out as particularly tragic and heroic. In 1867, five of the crew of thirteen were drowned going to the rescue of the schooner *Georgiana*. There is a plaque to the drowned men in the town church. In 1900 an even worse disaster saw eight crewmembers of the lifeboat *James Stevens no. 4* drown along with three members of the crew of *The Peace and Plenty*, the boat they were trying to rescue. A memorial to this tragedy can be found in the town cemetery.

For the local people of Padstow the lifeboat is hugely important. The sea provides an income for many people but she can be very dangerous and the brave volunteer lifeboat men provide a service to the town that everyone appreciates immensely. Every year the town has fund raising RNLI days when the air sea rescue helicopter, the main lifeboat and the inflatable rescue boats all put on a show. The egg rolling competition at Easter also raises money for the cause. In recent years the RNLI has taken over the training of the lifeguards that protect the public on the beaches during the holiday season. It is incredible to think that this rescue service is all funded by charitable donations. Next time you see a collection bucket dip into your pockets, you never know when you might need help.

The lifeboat launching from the station at Mother Ivey's Bay

autumn

Golden waves

fishing

Pilchards dominated the Cornish fishing industry for 500 years but during the last century they fell out of favour. Images of tins which were opened with keys to reveal fish in tomato sauce are the baby boomers' memory of pilchards. They are undergoing something of a renaissance, being relaunched as the Cornish sardine, a tasty summer dish for barbequing. Served with fresh crusty bread and a wedge of lemon they bring back memories of a Spanish holiday.

On the far side of the beach at Harlyn Bay stands an old Pilchard House. In the sixteenth to nineteenth centuries the fish were caught using a seine net. A huer would stand on the headland and look for enormous shoals of pilchards. Once he spotted them he would cry out alerting the fisherman of the fishes' presence. Two boats would row out carrying a net between them and surround the fish. They would row back to the beach with their catch and everyone from the village would help carry the catch to the house. There were often millions of fish in one catch. In 1868 there is was a record sixteen and a half million pilchards caught in one seine. Once in the house the fish were cleaned, gutted, salted and pressed and left for the oil to drip out into containers. This was evil, smelly work that was carried out by women and children. Once the fish were drained they were put in barrels or hogsheads and shipped to France, Spain and Italy. It was profitable for the owners of the Pilchard House but the workers were extremely poor. Above the window at the front of the house, carved in the stone lintel, are the words 'dulcis lucre odor' meaning 'profit smells sweet'. One consignment of hogsheads was shipped to Italy but returned unsold. Rather than give the fish to the starving locals the owner put it on the field behind the house as fertiliser. A local white witch, named Mother Ivey, had pleaded for the fish to be given to the people. She was so incensed by the owner's actions that she put a curse on the land. If anyone tried to cultivate the field they would be struck down – the field remains fallow to this day. This house is more famous today as the place where David Cameron holidayed with his family.

In Padstow in the second half of the nineteenth century drift netting took over from seining. The arrival of the railway at the turn of the nineteenth century was a huge boon. An ice factory was built next to the railway and fish were offloaded from the boats, packed in ice and sent by rail straight to Billingsgate market. The closure of the railway in the 1960s was a major blow to the fishermen.

Today most of the local fishermen have day boats that catch lobsters, crab and crayfish. They drop thousands of lobster pots to the sea bottom and check them daily for the tasty crustaceans. Their catch is offloaded in the harbour often into refrigerated trucks that drive straight to the continent. The Spanish in particular like the sweet flavoured spider crabs.

Other larger vessels also use the harbour. Both line-caught and trawled fish are offloaded and sent down to the big fish market at Newlyn. Over fifty varieties of fish are caught in Cornish waters and most are sold in the harbour fresh fish shops. There is nothing better than a crab sandwich for lunch and a wild sea bass fillet for supper. Treat yourself; you won't get better fresh fish anywhere.

OPPOSITE
LEFT Fishing with dad
RIGHT Digging for lugworms

LEFT Crabbers are the most common fishing boats in the harbour, usually owned by local fisherman
BELOW A big trawler pulls into the harbour to take refuge from heavy seas

Sand and sea

Sunrise over the Camel Estuary at Padstow

Big Autumn swells please
the surfers

prideaux place

The present residents of Prideaux Place are Peter and Elizabeth Prideaux-Brune. They moved there in 1988 and found a building and garden in need of much restoration. They set about the task with a vengeance and the house is now a wonderful example of a small stately home (a mere 81 rooms). It remains a family house, not just a museum, with many personal items lying around giving the place a very warm, lived in atmosphere.

The house has been continuously occupied by fourteen generations of the Prideaux family, since Elizabethan times. The family itself has been around in Cornwall even longer. The first Prideauxs date back to William the Conqueror. In fact Peter's son William is the Conqueror's great grandson twenty six times on.

The house was built by Sir Nicholas Prideaux in 1592. His portrait hangs above the fireplace in the dining room. When the portrait was originally painted he was just ordinary Nicholas Prideaux and his neck was bare. When he was knighted the painter returned to paint a ruff around his neck to signify that he was now nobility. The dining room also has some interesting carvings of figures on the panelling. The figures' arms move which is very unusual. It is not known why they were carved like this but a possible explanation is that different arm positions could send out secret messages to diners during the civil war.

The land on which the house is built was acquired for the family by the very astute great uncle of Sir Nicholas, his namesake Nicholas. He was an influential lawyer who persuaded the Prior of Bodmin to lease the monastic land to his niece very cheaply and so avoid having it seized by Henry VIII during the dissolution of the monasteries. Nicholas then suggested that his nephew should marry the Prior's niece. The marriage duly took place leaving the Prideaux family in charge of vast amounts of land including the area around Padstow. That land has remained in the family ever since.

In the Prideaux family history certain traits seem to stand out and reoccur. The choice of the law as their chosen profession is a continuous theme; the family has regularly produced very successful and influential lawyers. Political ineptitude leading them into dangerous alliances combined with an amazing ability to wriggle out of awkward situations and survive where others in similar situations perished is also a regular occurrence. They always seemed to support the wrong side in any major dispute, backing the King in The Civil War against Cromwell and Monmouth in his rebellion but when others lost their heads they managed to keep theirs. Lastly and possibly most importantly the men in the family regularly seem to marry very well.

The original house was Tudor, a classic e-shaped manor house, it remained untouched until the eighteenth century when Edmund Prideaux returned from Europe after completing his grand tour of the major cities on the continent. He updated the interior and was heavily influenced by the fashions of the day. In 1810 Edmund's grandson, the Reverend Charles, added the gothic wing to the southern aspect of the house. The present owners have restored a lot of the original features and paintings and are presently working on the gardens. In the grounds is the deer park believed to be the oldest in England and has been dated back to its enclosure by the Romans in 435AD.

The house is open to the public Sundays to Thursdays from Easter until October. There are regular guided tours by knowledgeable and entertaining guides and all the money raised goes on the upkeep and further restoration of this fascinating house.

OPPOSITE
LEFT The statue of 'The Boy with the Thorn' sits in the grounds of Prideaux Place overlooking the Camel Estuary
RIGHT Prideaux Place

RIGHT The fallow deer rut in the deer park (thought to be the oldest deer park in England).
BELOW Prideaux Place

A wreck on the beach near Pinkson Creek

The mudflats of Pinkson Creek exposed at low tide

Off to surf

Sand kiting at Tregloss

Sunset across Constantine Bay looking towards Trevose Head

betjeman and binyon

'It was above all Cornwall where he spent most of his youth and to which he annually returns that most deeply stirs this poet's senses . . . it excites him most in storm' so said Lord Birkenhead in his introduction to Sir John Betjeman's collected poems. Appropriately Betjeman was buried in St. Enodoc churchyard with the funeral service being conducted in gale force conditions. Mourners struggled with furious winds and pouring rain, conditions that would no doubt of appealed to the poet's sense of humour.

Many of his poems exhibited his sense of fun with lines such as 'sand in the sandwiches, wasps in the tea' being evocative of a family day out on the beach. It was this accessibility of his poetry that made him the most popular poet of his generation. Academics however weren't so enamoured with his work. Philip Larkin once said that 'The quickest way to start a punch up between two British literary critics is to ask them what they think of the poems of Sir John Betjeman'.

Betjeman was born in London and used to visit Cornwall every summer. His family at first rented and then owned a house in Daymer Lane, Trebetherick. The family would catch a train to Wadebridge and then take a horse and cart to their holiday destination. His experiences are captured in his autobiography *Summoned by Bells* with chapters IV and VIII dedicated to his childhood and adolescent years in Trebetherick.

At his first school in Highgate he was briefly taught by T.S.Elliot. He went on to study at Oxford where his tutor was C.S. Lewis, author of the Narnia Chronicles. There was no love lost between the two men with Lewis calling Betjeman an 'idle prig' and Betjeman not hiding his dislike of his eminent tutor. Whilst at Oxford he had a teddy called Archibald – a subject of one of his poems and the inspiration for Aloysius, Sebastian Flyte's teddy in *Brideshead Revisited*. Evelyn Waugh was a friend and contemporary at Oxford.

He left Oxford without a degree and much to his father's annoyance decided not to join the family firm. Instead he became a journalist, poet and broadcaster. He wrote for the *Evening Standard* as a film critic, wrote *Shell Guides* for tourists (one on Cornwall) and became Poet Laureate in 1972. He was passionate about railways and architecture, particularly Victorian architecture and campaigned against St. Pancras station being knocked down. Posthumously he was rewarded by having his statue put up in the newly re-vamped station.

He wrote many poems about his time in Cornwall including *Trebetherick*, *Cornish Cliffs*, *St. Enodoc* and *Seaside Golf*. He used to play golf (albeit badly) at the wonderful course at St. Enodoc. All bad golfers will understand the joy in his poem as he says:

'A glorious, sailing, bounding drive,
That made me glad I was alive.'

In 2006, his centenary year, there were events held in Polzeath and his life and works are celebrated at 'The John Betjeman Centre' in Wadebridge located appropriately in the refurbished Wadebridge station. In the summer there are occasionally poetry readings of his work held on the top of Bray Hill within sight of the beautiful churchyard of St. Enodoc where he is buried.

The other poet who used to frequent the area was Laurence Binyon. His name is not as well known as Betjeman's but one of his poems *For the Fallen* is possibly one of the best known poems in the world.

The words:

'They shall not grow old, as we that are left grow old
Age shall not weary them, nor the years condemn
At the going down of the sun and in the morning
We shall remember them.'

are spoken annually at remembrance services around the world in the UK, Canada, Australia and New Zealand. Binyon, a writer, academic and poet was too old to be called up to fight in the First World War so he volunteered to be a Red Cross medical orderly. He served the Red Cross on the Western Front where his experiences led him to write *For the Fallen*. On his return from the battlefields he sat on the cliff tops looking out over The Rumps and remembering the soldiers was inspired to write the verse that is still so evocative today.

There is a plaque on the coast path where he sat and wrote the poem with the verse etched in the stone. It is emotional to read the verse looking out over the stunning view of The Rumps and the North Cornish coast.

CLOCKWISE FROM TOP LEFT John Betjeman's grave,
The memorial stone on the coast path near The Rumps, St. Enodoc Church

John
Betjeman
1906-1984

FOR THE FALLEN
Composed on these cliffs, 1914
They shall grow not old, as we that are left grow old:
Age shall not weary them, nor the years condemn.
At the going down of the sun and in the morning
We will remember them.
Laurence Binyon (1869 - 1943)
Dedicated 14.9.2003

OPPOSITE Surfers emerge from the sea at dusk

ABOVE AND LEFT The setting sun as seen from Pentire Farm, Polzeath

The Camel Estuary at dawn

The obelisk celebrating Queen Victoria's Jubilee, at sunrise

Egloshayle Church at dawn

the lobster hatchery

There was a time not so long ago that lobsters on the Maine coast of America were so plentiful that they were washed ashore in their thousands and were considered food fit only for the poor. In Europe they have always been considered a delicacy but what unites the American and European lobsters is the decline in both their numbers.

The National Lobster Hatchery was set up in 2002 to counteract this decline. Local fishermen bring in pregnant lobsters to the hatchery where they are put in tanks until they give birth. These pregnant lobsters release up to 10,000 eggs into the tank usually over several nights. The eggs are collected and put into a special tank full of swirling water saturated in plankton. In these ideal conditions the little lobster eggs grow quickly and moult their skin regularly and soon begin to look like miniature versions of their parents. At this stage they are removed from the tank and put into individual cells to prevent them from cannibalising each other (a habit that captive lobsters are prone too). After three months the tiny lobsters are released into the sea. Having raised them to this stage their survival rates are significantly higher than if the lobster had just laid her eggs directly into the sea. Less than one percent of the larvae survive to this stage in the wild compared with around forty percent in the hatchery.

Lobsters are loners, living solitary lives, meeting other lobsters only to mate. The females can only mate when they are moulting. They shed their shell and when particularly vulnerable to being eaten have to approach aggressive males that could easily gobble them up. Luckily for the females more often than not the males are more interested in the sex on offer than the food. After mating the female stays hidden until her shell has hardened and it is safe to venture forth. Pregnancy for a female lobster is a long, protracted affair. She stores the sperm, sometimes for months, until she is ready to lay the eggs. When the eggs are eventually laid they nestle in her tail held there by a special sort of secreted glue. The eggs remain in her tail for nine to eleven months until it is time for them to be set free to take their chances in the dangerous sea.

Many aspects of the lobster's life and biology are really quite bizarre. They have three stomachs, the first of which contains teeth with which to crush the shells of its prey. Its legs are sensory organs covered in taste bud-like structures so that a lobster can be said to taste with its feet. They can live to be over a hundred years old continually moulting their old shell and growing into their new one. The largest lobster caught in Cornwall was found in Falmouth in 1931 and it measured 1.26m long. It is strange to think such a peculiar creature can taste so good!

The Lobster Hatchery plays an important role in the restocking of the area with new young viable lobsters so hopefully the fishermen can continue making a living from catching them and we can continue to enjoy their tasty meat. The hatchery is an interesting place to visit to check out the weird and wonderful world of the lobster.

OPPOSITE Baby, teenage and fully grown lobsters

BELOW Lobsters ready for export

OVERLEAF Walking on the beach at sunset

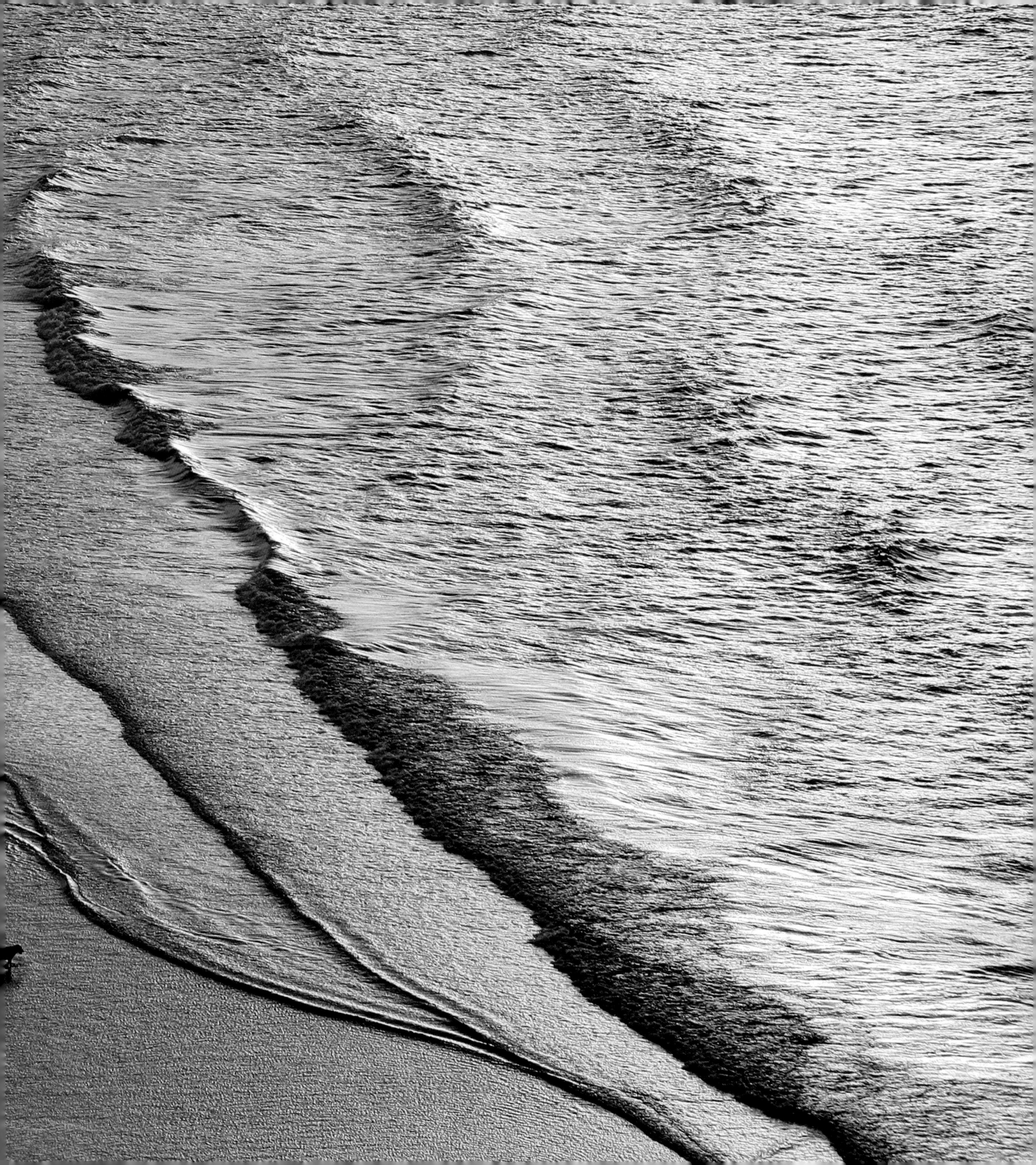

Two fabulous linx golf clubs at Trevose and St. Enodoc

Great bird watching on the Amble Marshes

Two for the price of one: the retreating tide leaves a thin layer of water on the beach which acts like a mirror reflecting the beautiful skies

Beautiful Harlyn Bay at sunset

index